Abigail E. Weeks
Memorial Library
Union College

presented by

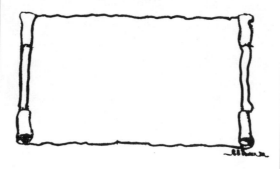

ALL COLOUR BOOK OF
ART DECO

DAN KLEIN   Photographs by Angelo Hornak

Octopus
Octopus Books

CONTENTS

INTRODUCTION

'In olden days a glimpse of stocking was looked on as something shocking, but now God knows anything goes'
Cole Porter

ETHEL MERMAN sang this Cole Porter song in 1934, and the refrain mirrors a frenzied world recovering from the crippling effects of one war and speeding towards another. "Anything goes" is a catch-phrase that neatly captures the spirit of Art Deco, the name that is now fast becoming a household word to describe every kind of decorative design between the wars. It has the advantage of being a convenient international term differing only in pronunciation from country to country, but it can lead to endless confusion as it covers so many schools of design. Both a carved sycamore chair by Paul Follot, romantically decorated with flowers and fruit, and a chaise longue by Le Corbusier with a chromium-plated steel tube frame can pass for Art Deco. It is merely the loosest coat-hanger word coined after an exhibition held in Paris in 1966 called 'Les Années '25'; that exhibition concentrated on the 'twenties and the famous 1925 Paris 'Exposition Internationale des Arts Décoratifs et Industriels Modernes'. In 1969 Studio Vista published Bevis Hillier's book, 'Art Deco', and in 1971 the Minneapolis Institute of Arts organized an exhibition called 'The World of Art Deco', which included decorative design of the 'thirties. Now for better or worse we are stuck with the term; it is meant to evoke a panorama of flat-chested flappers dancing the Charleston in the latest cocktail dresses from Paris, of interior decoration smothered with floral patterns, of the geometry of Odeon cinemas, or of chrome and glass furniture. Some sorting out is necessary before the images become too confused and kaleidoscopic.

The designers working between the wars can be divided into two broad categories; the sybarites who covered every available surface with their new stylized flowers and fruit, and the revolutionaries who wanted purity of line uncluttered by decoration and who turned to the aesthetics of machinery for inspiration. The first group, consisted mainly of Paris fashion designers and interior decorators, extravagantly led by Paul Poiret, the second revolved around the various avant-guarde schools of architecture and their leaders; and

in particular the Swiss-born architect, philosopher and designer, Le Corbusier, who claimed that a house should be a "machine for living in". But one concept was common to all Art Deco designers, that of total design. Whether you wished your house to look like clockwork or like an exotic jungle, every detail from the keyhole to the radiator grille was worthy of the designer's attention. This has greatly affected the survival rate of complete Art Deco buildings. Some of the most important Art Deco design went into the building of factories, but the enormous changes in the world of industry have made it impossible to preserve them. On the other hand, with such attention to every sort of design, a great many items of interest remain, and the hunt for Art Deco is never ending.

'So we came to the Ritz Hotel and the Ritz Hotel is devine. Because when a girl can sit in a delightful bar and have delicious champagne cocktails and look at all the important French people in Paris, I think it is devine, I mean when a girl can sit there and look at the Dolly Sisters . . . . .'
Anita Loos – Gentlemen Prefer Blondes

PARIS led the world of fashion during the 1920s, and as the Art Deco movement was largely initiated and inspired by fashion designers, all eyes turned to Paris for the '1920s look'. From 1915 till 1925 Paul Poiret was the undisputed dictator not only of what women should wear, but also of the decor that would best complement the clothes he designed. His colours and designs were strongly influenced by Diaghilev's Ballets Russes, and in looking for a beginning to Art Deco most art historians agree that the movement was born in 1909, when that year Diaghilev brought his Russian dance company to Paris for the first time. The explosion of colour and the boldness of design that the Parisians saw during that season brought an end to the delicate tendrils and curves of the Art Nouveau period. Flowers became formalized and geometric; perhaps the clearest example of the transition from whiplash tendrils to geometric rosebuds can be seen in the designs of Charles Rennie Mackintosh, the Scottish architect, painter and designer, who stripped Art Nouveau design

of gratuitous ornament and pointed the way to the cleaner lines of Art Deco. There were other favourite Art Deco motifs besides the flower; for instance fountains, leaping gazelles and, as geometry took over, sunbursts and lightning ziggurats. The discovery of Tutankhamen's tomb in 1923 made the Egyptian influence predominant for a while. By the 'thirties the geometrical shapes that had made animals, flowers and plants look angular gained the upper hand and became decorations in themselves; a "brave new world of unforeseen technological advance" made the aesthetics of machinery fashionable and pure geometry became the decorative mania of the 'thirties. In amongst all this, traces of Fauvism, Cubism, Futurism or Negro art were to be found. Art Deco designers borrowed freely; they made decorative use of every new invention but were rarely innovators themselves. Rather was the movement led by "fashion stylists, graphics designers, craftsmen or theorists whose prime concern was with taste and style rather than with practicality and performance".

'Take a tuck in that skirt Isabel, it's 1925'
Anita Loos

FOR a while the novelty of Art Deco lay in the fact that it was dominated by the designers of the fashion world. There were various reasons for this, perhaps the most important being that during the 'twenties fashion became big business; a wider market was made possible by greatly improved communications throughout the world. Even Poiret, the king of 'haute-couture', lectured on the advantages of mass-production and the joys of ready-to-wear dresses. These clothes were worn by a new type of woman who emerged after World War I with the new-found independence she had won by working while the men were away at the front fighting. Poiret helped her to express her freedom by freeing her from the corset and completely changing her shape; his dictates were taken seriously, and the latest dress-style was of the greatest importance. Fashion designers exploited women's weakness for new clothes by changing styles and colours as often as possible; there was talk of fever-chart hemlines as dress lengths shot up and down. Waistlines travelled too, from below the bust to below the navel. But certain things stand out as distinguishing marks of the Art Deco period, such as cloche hats, bandeaux worn immediately above the eyebrows, short cropped hair (which became softer, slightly longer and more wavy in the 'thirties), 'cupid's bow' mouths and the complete disappearance of the bust. Certain colours, too, evoke the 'twenties and 'thirties, like tango (a burnt orange shade that took its name from the popular tea dance), silver and black.

Just as important as the clothes were the accessories, perfumes and make-up that accompanied them. Poiret set the fashion by marketing his own perfume; Jeanne Lanvin, Chanel, Coty and Worth followed suit. The women's magazines published articles re-assuring their readers (particularly unmarried women) that make-up, if discreetly used, was not sinful. Modernist dressing-tables became the focal point of the bedroom, a new sort of shrine to beauty. Great care was taken over the packaging of cosmetics, particularly perfumes, and the best glass designers like Baccarat and Lalique were employed to design scent bottles. Lalique also designed

a face powder box for Coty. Jewellery was either very expensive from Cartier, Boucheron or van Cleef & Arpels, or unashamedly false. Chromium and the newly invented bakelite (which was made in a variety of splendid colours) were used for costume jewellery; the more exclusive pieces were couturier designed, but much of it was simply mass-produced. Bakelite was considered exotic enough to be used with precious stones and precious metals even by Cartier. Brightly coloured enamels in jazzy designs were also very popular, and some of the enamelled cigarette cases, powder compacts, buckles and brooches of that period were beautifully designed and have become collectors' items today. And in true Art Deco style, even accessories like handbags, scarves and shoes paid the greatest possible attention to decorative brilliance.

'Poor child! Her little cartier diamond bracelet flashed in the sunlight as she released the brake of her car and, as she sped away, I thought 'clever Noel Coward' Poor little rich girl indeed'
Angus Wilson – For Whom The Cloche Tolls

POOR Little Rich Girl! In America she was called "the flapper", in Italy "La Maschietta", in France "La Garçonne".

However you described her, she set the mood for the 'twenties. "The free and easy boy girl with shingled hair, a cigarette, a driving licence." Mrs Pankhurst and the suffragettes had started the fight to liberate women and World War I accelerated their emancipation. They began working in jobs that had hitherto been filled exclusively by men and began to make their mark in the business world, particularly the business of interior decoration, fashion and decorative art. Many of the famous designers in Europe, America and England were women. There had been women designers in the Art Nouveau movement, but they were far less involved in the commercial aspect; apart from anything else Art Nouveau was an arts and crafts movement that deplored the machine; Art Deco used the newest possible machinery to make good craftsmanship available to the general public. It was a case of supply and demand, for new fortunes had been acquired during World War I and the re-distribution of wealth brought forward a large clientele with new tastes and a new type of home to furnish. The richest of the 'nouveaux riches' had plenty of money to spend, but many of them did not trust their own taste. After the war they found themselves with money but no position in society; 'Studio' magazine referred to them as "the present possessors of great

L'ECHO DE PARIS

L'ECHO DE PARIS

6

wealth . . . . a different and on the whole less cultured class". Many members of this new moneyed class were starting from scratch. They wished to achieve a total new look that concealed humble beginnings, and the best way was often to employ the services of an interior decorator. A few people were willing to spend vast sums of money on their homes and a few designers, like Emile-Jacques Ruhlmann, catered for their needs. Ruhlmann's furniture was the height of luxury, "veneers of rare woods, amaranthe, violet-wood, macassar ebony, encrusted with ivories and materials like morocco leather and sharkskin". His 'Pavillon d'un Collectionneur' at the 1925 Paris Exhibition won the highest praise and admiration, and today his furniture is to be found in museums and important private collections. But Ruhlmann was something of an exception and the costly workmanship that went into his furniture a hangover from a bygone age.

The new middle class wanted elegant homes that were easy to run – sumptuous mansions with liveried servants belonged to another era. Modern chic made a completely new set of demands on designers and decorators. Households were becoming smaller, but everything in the home had to be a witness to taste and style. As space became more limited, every bit became a vital living area. Kitchens were no longer confined to dark basements staffed with cooks and maids. Self-respecting citizens spent time in them and it was important that they should be pleasantly designed and practical. Bathrooms took on a completely new look, with streamlined fittings and new labour-saving floor and wall coverings in jazzy designs. No decorative detail was free from comment or criticism in fashion journals and magazines devoted to interior decoration.

As entertaining became more of a problem, formal dinner parties gave way to cocktail parties; a whole new society cult was born and of course the clothes, accessories and furniture to go with it. Modernist cocktail cabinets were given pride of place; cocktail accessories became as ridiculous as the small-talk that accompanied those new drinks. Asprey made a cocktail shaker in the shape of a dumb bell; Ronson made a monkey lighter and cigarette dispenser combined – at the touch of a lever an Art Deco monkey bends over to pick up a cigarette out of a metal container. Kitsch was in its element at the cocktail bar.

'I designed innumerable dresses and coats, accessories such as hats, head-dresses, gloves, shoes, muffs, fans and masks and many other objects for interior decoration, chairs, screens, light-fittings, cushions, vases, what have I not designed. Even bath-towels'
Erté

THE ever increasing ranks of the middle classes were preoccupied with taste and kept designers busy. They considered it safer to invest in the proven design talents of others to decorate their homes than to be branded as tasteless. Poiret attracted the richest if not the classiest members of society to his gardens and salons with his 'masked balls of Neronian pomp'. The balls were meant as more than pure entertainment; they were a shop window for Poiret's exuberant tastes, and significant because they were designed specifically to show off the decorative arts, which the general public were only too anxious to buy for themselves. Poiret also formed a design studio known as L'Atelier Martine, in 1911. For a while Raoul Dufy collaborated with him over this and Poiret made use of other first-class, though as yet unknown artists. The studio was chiefly for the production of carpets and hand-woven or hand-printed textiles. As a commercial venture it failed (partly because Dufy left), but it set the fashion for design studios.

Industrialists began to appreciate the value of good design, and the big department stores in Paris, realizing the business potential of interior decoration, employed famous designers to open departments for them. Louis Sue and André Mare started the Compagnie des Arts, which provided well-designed furniture at reasonable prices; Paul Follot worked for Bon Marché; Marcel Dufrène for Galleries Lafayette, and at Printemps there was L'Atelier Primavera. All these workshops prided themselves on having a distinctive style and competed with each other for excellence of design. Other European capitals followed the example set by Paris. London was slowest of all, and it was only after a decade of complaints by enlightened writers in 'Studio' magazine:

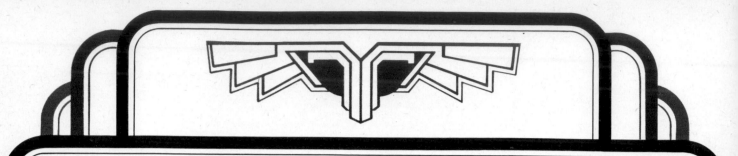

("it is unfortunate that the patterns displayed in most of the shops are so extraordinarily dull and commonplace," 'Studio', 1924) that Waring and Gillow went modern with a department for French furniture under the direction of Serge Chermayeff. The best English furniture in the 'twenties and 'thirties was that sold at Heal's, some of it designed by Sir Ambrose Heal; but excellent as it was, this belonged more in spirit to the Arts and Crafts movement of earlier decades. It was not till the very late 'twenties and early 'thirties that English interior decoration developed a recognizable and interesting style. In America there was plenty of money, particularly before the Wall Street crash in 1929, but according to Paul Frankl (remembered best for his 'skyscraper furniture'), the general public was quite unconscious of the fact that modern art had been extended into the field of business and industry. Frankl wrote: "The only reason why America was not represented in Paris 1925 was because we found we had no decorative art". By 1929 this was no longer true with sumptuously furnished

buildings like Radio City Music Hall where Donald Deskey was responsible for the sheer fantasy of every aspect of interior decoration, or William van Alen's glittering Chrysler building, or the Chanin building with Jacques Delamarre's amazing radiator grilles, elevator doors, theatre on the 52nd floor and friezes in Atlantic terracotta and bronze adorning the outside of the building. Interior decorators opened up offices in New York and were kept extremely busy. It was a profession which many of the newly emancipated women considered suitable and not too shocking. The best known of American lady designers, Elsie de Wolfe, had designed the Colony Club as early as 1905, and was later commissioned by Frick to decorate an entire floor of his 5th Avenue mansion. In England and America Syrie Maugham, the wife of the author, excited comment with her white interiors but was criticized for going too far when she coated valuable Georgian furniture in white paint to tone in with her schemes. Interior decoration became big business and there was much money to be made from it.

'While painting in the Salon D'Automne makes no advance . . . . while sculpture remains where it is . . . . decorative art continues its sure progress and captivates visitors' interest. It is only receiving its just due. Without any doubt decorative art is harvesting the fruits of experience and it is mainly of cubism that we are thinking, formerly only cultivated in the realms of pure and disinterested art. Now it is the 'Modern Man's Office', which holds the attention of the exhibitors and designers: another time the 'Private Cocktail Bar', 'The Dining Room' or 'The Living Room'.'
Studio Magazine, 1931

THERE were two important developments which affected living accommodation after World War I. First of all, with smaller apartments, every bit of space was valuable and had to be carefully designed. Then there was the important link between art and industry, which opened up a whole new field for designers. Factories were no longer a blot on the landscape with chimneys belching smoke. Where possible the ugly mechanics of production were hidden behind streamlined façades, as for instance in the Hoover building at Perivale, just outside London. Executive

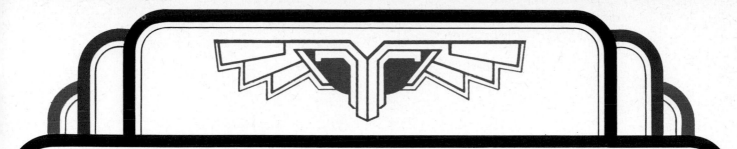

offices had to flatter the taste and personality of the executives using them and interior decorators were called in to create a suitably impressive look. In the home, kitchens and bathrooms became the decorator's new playground; technological advance was complemented wherever possible by the designer's creative talents. Particular attention was paid to lighting, and new inventions like radios or electric fires took on the craziest disguises. One of the illustrations in this book shows a sailing-ship fire, another a radio in a lacquered 'chinoiserie' case. As far as lighting was concerned, there was an endless variety of chandeliers, wall fittings and decorative lamps; some showing off the amazing skills of glass manufacturers like Lalique or Argy Rousseau, some the superb metalwork of Edgar Brandt or Majorelle. The most functional of objects became decorative.

It has not been possible in a short book to include illustrations of the work of all the great designers of the 'twenties and 'thirties. For instance there is no illustration of Puiforcat's silver, of Sonia Delaunay's textiles, of Rosenthal porcelain or of Décorchemont 'pâte de verre' glass. On the other hand there are illustrations by lesser craftsmen or designers, because a great part of the charm of Art Deco lies in unimportant ephemeral items like the 'Savoy Cocktail Book' or a mass-produced plastic inkwell. Many of the illustrations show the work of English designers, partly because it was easily accessible but mainly because the restrained English Deco look has been eclipsed by the flashy French look and has not yet had the appreciation it deserves.

'Since a poster is a way of addressing a hurried passer-by, already harrassed by a jumble of images of every kind, it must provoke surprise, rape his sensibility and mark his memory with an indelible print'
**Posters & their Designers –
Studio Special Number, 1924**

SPEED and publicity were the two important aspects of the modern world of the 'twenties. Cars, aeroplanes, trains and travel were in the news, and on the artist's mind. Both Le Corbusier and Ruhlmann made attempts at designing cars. Yvonne Brunhammer in her book on Art Deco sees the aeroplane and the automobile

designed "in new forms taken over from cubism and its successors". Travel was the subject of many decorative panels (like the painted ceiling in the lobby of the Chrysler building). Ocean liners became floating museums, particularly the 'Ile de France' and the 'Normandie' where the interior decoration was done by a distinguished team of craftsmen and designers; on the 'Normandie' (launched in 1932) the main dining room had walls lined with hammered glass panels and two gigantic chandeliers by Lalique; the lounge had four decorative panels by Dupas, and there was furniture by Ruhlmann in some of the better suites. The French government encouraged such extravagance as being the best possible publicity for the luxury arts and crafts, and money invested in publicity during the 'twenties and 'thirties was considered well spent.

Improved communications opened up undreamed-of export markets; people moved faster and further than ever before and it became increasingly important to advertise. In a special number of the 'Studio' in 1924 devoted entirely to advertising, the editor says: "This is the day of the poster. Some of the best brains in the business world of today are concentrated on the possibilities of the poster as a means for advancing trade and the services of the most skilful artists are requisitioned to forward the desired end," – artists like McKnight Kauffer and Frank Brangwyn in England, Cassandre and Jean Dupas in France, Van Dongen in Holland. In England the railway companies (including London Transport) commissioned some of the best posters, with "instantaneous appeal, and the story truthfully stated in language so simple that the real meaning cannot be misconstrued". The 1924 'Studio' special poster number concludes: "Poster designers are producing some of the most outstanding work of our time." These designers worked not only on posters, but on advertisements in magazines, on wrappers, labels, booklets, prospectuses, and letter headings.

'Studio' brought out another special number in 1925 devoted to Art and Publicity and here the editor appraises the importance of advertising: "The old days have passed, and with them have gone the old-time manufacturers, merchants and tradesmen who lived and worked on their own premises, the craftsmen and

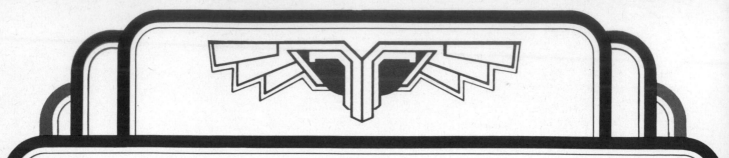

prentices, and the travellers who journeyed by coach; the conditions they knew have long ceased to be and have crumbled before the forward march of progress, production on a huge scale, collective bargaining, the coming of the large store, the rise of the trade unions, and business activities embracing the whole world. Nowhere have the effects of this transformation been more apparent than in the direction of advertising and printing. Printed advertising has advanced with the times, and in recent years to so marked a degree, that it now occupies a higher place in everyday affairs then it has ever reached before." Although the benefits of advertising were universally agreed upon, there were still complaints that businessmen too frequently failed to appreciate the value of good design and failed to realise that "such homely subjects as bacon, eggs, syrup, shirts and socks or glue" could acquire new glamour in the hands of a good artist. But there were a few firms that believed in using artistic talents to promote their merchandise, firms like Bon Marché in Paris, Wesson Oil in America, or Eastman Dyers and Cleaners in England. Their advertisements are admired forty years after they were done and continue to influence poster art and graphic design today.

'The great life of the machine has shaken Society, has snapped all chains, opened all doors, and cast its eyes in every direction'
Le Corbusier

SO far most of the decorators and designers mentioned have been those who catered for middle-class tastes and the middle-brow intellect; these artists and craftsmen asked no searching questions about social reform, nor did they concern themselves with the deeper implications of changes in modern society. Not so Le Corbusier, whose all-white pavilion at Expo '25 was meant as a protest against the surfeit of prettiness on display in other pavilions. The pavilion was called 'L'Esprit Nouveau' and did all it could to break with tradition and to bend people's minds towards a modern way of life and a new aesthetic. Le Corbusier was a severe critic of the 1925 Exhibition and made his protest in strong terms. "We protest in the name of everything. In the name of happiness and well-being, in the name

of good taste . . . . . it is said that decoration is necessary to our existence. Let us correct that. Art is necessary to us, that is to say, it is a disinterested passion which elevates us." These words stab straight at the heart of Art Deco, the art of decorating and ornamenting every available surface. Le Corbusier was not alone in his attack. Many other schools in Europe combined philosophy and architecture and deeply mistrusted the attempts of the 'nouveaux .riches' at building over-decorated fortresses to shut out the problems of the real world.

In Holland Van Doesburg edited the forward-looking magazine 'De Stijl' from 1917 to 1931; he and his followers were interested in finding forms to express the newness of twentieth-century experience, "to construct without any illusion, without any decoration, is one of the principal aims of the Stijl movement". Perhaps the most compact expression of the ideals of this school is to be found in a wooden chair by Rietveld. It is an amazing 'construction' preoccupied with the arrangement of material in space, an experiment to express philosophy in a chair. The result looks most uncomfortable, but this was no easy-chair designed to cosset the rich. The chair was meant to keep the sitter "physically and mentally toned up".

In Germany Walter Gropius had established the Bauhaus a few months after the end of World War I. During the fourteen years of its existence, intellectuals, artists and craftsmen (Gropius, Klee, Breuer, Feininger, Kandinsky, Moholy-Nagy) fought with and against each other to express their own brand of modernism.

In Italy the Futurist movement under the leadership of the poet Marinetti published manifesto after manifesto in high-flown rhetoric. "There is no more beauty except in strife. No masterpiece without aggressiveness . . . . . we shall sing of the great crowds in the excitement of labour, pleasure and rebellion; of the multi-coloured and polyphonic surf of revolutions in modern capital cities; of the nocturnal vibrations of arsenals and work-shops beneath their violent electric moons; of greedy stations swallowing smoking snakes; of factories suspended from the clouds by their strings of smoke; of bridges leaping like gymnasts . . . . of broad-chested locomotives prancing the rails like huge steel horses

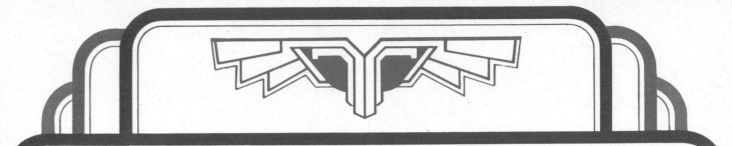

.... and of the gliding flight of aeroplanes, the sound of whose screws is like the flapping of flags and the applause of an enthusiastic crowd." This 'cri de coeur' seems far removed from the happy exuberance of Paul Poiret and the unquestioning fun of Paris fashion. Although the ideals expressed by these various schools seem a long way away from the gentle art of decoration, it is important to mention them in a book about Art Deco. Le Corbusier, Marinetti and Van Doesburg were working at the same time as Lalique, Ruhlmann, Poiret or Sonia Delaunay. The work of the philosopher artists helps to put the work of the fashion designers and interior decorators into perspective. Moreover, although Art Deco designers had neither the time nor the inclination to stop and listen to the impassioned outbursts of the moderns, the evolution of their style owed a lot to the innovators in the enemy camp. After the Paris Exhibition of 1925 the rash of ornamentation subsided and decorative art became simpler. Aldous Huxley in his "Notes on Decoration" published in 'Studio' Magazine in 1930 sums up the fusion of opposing elements: "The contemporary style has evolved out of the harsh artistic puritanism of a cubism which, in its first violent reaction against the prettinesses would suffer nothing but straight lines and angles, into something more ripe and humane .... whether we like it or not, we have actually grown to prefer the simplicities. We have tempered them, however, with a certain graciousness of form."

'Cocktails and laughter but what comes after?'
Noel Coward

WHEN did Art Deco end? Why did it end? What followed it? There isn't really any answer to these questions – Art Deco was never a specific movement. Futurism began and ended with Marinetti; De Stijl died with Van Doesburg, but decorative art muddled its way through thick and thin. In a sense it has never ended; it merely progressed on a tortuous route changing its look every now and again when a new designer came along, and a new trend was set. Some authors have made Art Deco end with the Wall Street crash in 1929. Certainly

there were great changes after that; depression was in the air, but in some cases this led to a show of extravagance for appearance's sake (one thinks of luxury skyscrapers standing half empty during the Depression – the Empire State building was renamed the Empty State Building). However, the simplicity of the 'thirties design did not really signify hard times; as Aldous Huxley said in the 'Studio' 1930: "Simplicity of form contrasts at the present time with richness of materials and has invented many new materials to work on. Modern simplicities are rich and sumptuous; we are Quakers whose severely cut clothes are made of damask and cloth of silver." In 1933 Donald Deskey, who designed the interior of Radio City Music Hall, wrote: "From the chaotic situation arising out of an era of prosperity without precedent for decoration, produced by Expo '25 in Paris .... a style emerged ... one lot of motives was simply substituted for another ... ornamental syntax consisted almost entirely of a few motifs such as the zigzag, the triangle, fawn-like curves and designs". Between the wars changes in ornamental syntax occurred with great frequency, which made for an enormous variety of styles, but also makes the task of defining Art Deco a very difficult one. Art Deco is a thousand different styles, the ever changing look of the decorative arts of the 'twenties and 'thirties. The illustrations that follow can only serve as an introduction to a vast area of design, decoration, ornamentation and fantasy.

musique

LEFT
"Speed was a novelty. The 1920s were intoxicated by it, but had no presentiment of the way in which it was to revolutionize life. The aeroplane and the automobile were designed in new forms taken over from cubism and its successors" (Yvonne Brunhammer: 'The Nineteen-twenties style'). Le Corbusier and Ruhlmann designed cars; Sonia Delaunay and Maurice Dufrène both decorated motorcars in bright cubist patterns. Lalique designed car mascots. Speed created a new excitement to which artists responded eagerly. In the illustration it finds its way into the design for a headscarf, as streamlined racing cars streak through stylized clouds.

ABOVE
Half-title page designed by Natalia Gontcharova for 'Le Poisson d'Or', a poem and piano piece composed by Lord Berners; published by J & W Chester in 1919. Gontcharova was one of the designers used by Diaghilev, whose Ballets Russes took Paris by storm when the company gave its first season there in 1909. Diaghilev caused a revolution not only with his new dance techniques, but in scenic art too through Bakst and his collaborators. Paris saw a whole new colour spectrum in their designs which in turn started a revolution in decorative design of every sort.

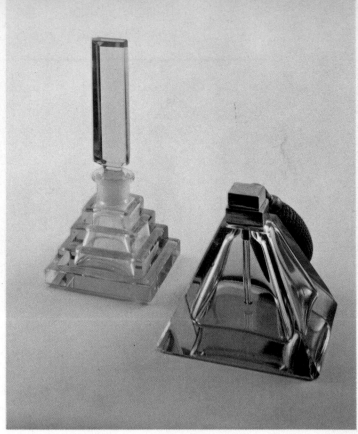

ABOVE

Chrome and glass table-lamp with gilded spelter lady. Although this is a mass-produced object, it is charmingly designed and well made. By the 1920s the wonders of electricity were taken for granted, designers found light-fittings a new and inspiring challenge. Lights had either to be completely hidden or be made decorative. We find everything from streamlined chrome, poised dancing ladies in porcelain, bronze or spelter, condemned like lost souls in Hades to support globes of light until the glass got smashed or the ladies were put away in cupboards by a new generation who found them vulgar.

TOP RIGHT

It is generally agreed that American Indian art and particularly the stepped shape of Aztec temples had a considerable influence on design in the 'twenties. This is particularly noticeable in some skyscrapers of the period (for instance the Empire State Building in New York), in furniture design, "even in things as unsacred as radio-sets" (Bevis Hillier – 'The World of Art Deco'). The above illustration shows two scent bottles, ordinary mass-produced objects whose shape must surely have been inspired by American Indian pyramids, or tombs of Old Mexico.

ABOVE

Small desk or table watch by Meyrowitz (of London and New York) in silver gilt and enamel; the numerals are unmistakably '20s as is the green sun-ray enamelling on the face of the watch, but the stongest part of the designs is in the scarab-wing sides showing Egyptian influence. After Tutankhamen's tomb was discovered in 1923 Egyptian motifs appeared in designs of every sort: one of the best examples was in Graumann's Egyptian Theater on Hollywood Boulevard where the stage "made King Tut's tomb look like the old family burial vault".

RIGHT

Ziggurats, cubes, geometric flowers and leaves, silver, all the symbols and signs of French Art Deco here combine to make a glorious silk evening scarf. Nothing is known about the designer or manufacturer, but the sheer extravagance and assurance of design suggest one of the Paris fashion houses. Paris fashion had no conscience about borrowing from an art movement or from the work of a particular painter whose colour palette or design might translate successfully into fabric. Motifs from the Ballets Russes, from Cubism or from the Fauve painters all found their way into fashion design. Also during the 'twenties painters were commissioned to design for fashion houses.

ABOVE
Design by Léon Bakst for the costume of Potiphar's wife in the ballet "La Légende de Joseph", for which the music was by Richard Strauss. Léon Bakst (1886 – 1924) was the chief designer for Diaghilev's Ballets Russes when this company gave its first season in Paris in 1909. With their costumes and scenery, Bakst and his collaborators brought about a revolution in the history of scenic art, which in turn revolutionized Paris fashion, introducing a new colour spectrum, new shapes, a completely new look. Paul Poiret introduced this look into the Paris fashion world; the new colours had liberated him from "an atmosphere of 18th century refinement", and he says "Now I have let some wolves into the sheepfold, those lively reds, greens, purples and blues make all the rest sit up".

LEFT
This soup tureen comes from a dinner service by Spode called 'Royal Jasmine' and dates from the 1930s. The sparse geometry of the decoration shows a complete reaction against the busy flowers and festoons that were among the more popular motifs of the 'twenties. Clean lines, partly inspired by the cubist painters, partly by Le Corbusier's purist philosophy of design were used for decoration. Basic shapes (like the square, the triangle and the circle) and their spatial arrangements greatly interested the designers of the 'thirties. Silver, cream and apple-green were colours that were very much in vogue for interior decoration.

PREVIOUS PAGE
'Miss Modern' of the early 1930s would be wearing one of the new 'tailored frocks' perhaps trimmed with chromium buttons (the latest thing in 'smart notions'), a bangle (worn above the elbow with a handkerchief slipped through it) and a necklace in chromium and bakelite might complete the outfit. There were novelty necklaces of all sorts from "ordinary common or garden tap washers with big marble-like beads in any gay colour as a contrast – whoever could guess – ?" to the most sophisticated Bauhaus-inspired all-aluminium jewellery. It was a comparative novelty that all this jewellery was unashamedly 'false'. The dancing figure from which the necklaces are hung is by the Austrian sculptor Lorenzl.

LEFT
Detail of a very long paste, jade and silver necklace and pendant, probably French and dating from the mid-'twenties. Long strings of beads were a vital fashion accessory in the 'twenties and went well with the flat-fronted look. This is a more dressy and infinitely more expensive version of the long dangling necklace and meant for evening wear. The links are beautifully articulated so as to follow the line and movement of the body. The necklace would come down to about the navel of a woman of average height. Paste and diamanté settings came very much back into fashion during the 'twenties, but one rarely finds a piece as superbly made as this.

BELOW
Wallpaper by Donald Deskey in the second mezzanine men's lounge of Radio City Music Hall, New York. The theme depicted is "Nicotine"; the paper is printed in tobacco brown on aluminium foil paper. The American designer Donald Deskey was in charge of the overall interior decoration of Radio City Music Hall, and designed much of the splendid furniture and many of the accessories that help to turn it into the 'Art Deco' monument that it is today. The building was designed by Rockefeller Center Inc. architects, and it was they who chose Deskey to assist in the furnishing and decoration of the building.

RIGHT
Two of a set of six fashion plates for the Parisian Furrier Simon Frères. With artists such as Poiret and Erté doing fashion designs, fashion drawing became a highly cultivated art. Erté designed for 'La Gazette du bon ton', for 'Vogue', and was associated regularly with 'Harper's Bazaar' for 22 years. The designs illustrated are probably from around 1929. Martin Battersby in 'The Decorative Twenties' describes the fashion in that winter: "small and head-hugging hats were worn with the huge fur collars, collars which often continued as a border round the hem of the coat which was invariably three-quarter length". The greyhound seems almost to have become a fashion accessory during the 1920s.

BELOW RIGHT
A collection of clips and buckles, some in bakelite and some enamelled. Belt buckles and clips came under the heading of 'utility jewellery', they were immensely popular, and as the term suggests, very useful. An issue of 'Woman's Own' in the early 'thirties devotes an entire article to clips. A clip could be worn in a beret, "but that doesn't mean it won't look equally well in a simple felt hat, clipped a little to the left of the centre front of the band. Again, if you had two they'd be the perfect finish to a pair of plain satin shoes for your evening frock. As for the really lovely effect on a black chiffon velvet evening-bag – well, words couldn't describe it!"

SÎMON FRÈRES
SOCIÉTÉ ANONYME AU CAPITAL DE 10.000.000 DE FRANCS

FOURRURES & PELLETERIES
EN GROS

PARIS
5, RUE GEOFFROY-MARIE
TÉL. LOUVRE 04-01
PROVENCE 02-88 02-34

LONDRES
MIDLAND BANK CHAMBERS MARKET PLACE OXFORD CIRCUS
TÉL. MUSEUM 31-66

BRUXELLES
42, BOULEVARD DU JARDIN BOTANIQUE
TÉL. 117-77
R.C. SEINE 217.609

TOP
Hand-printed silk with bold design where hot shades of red and purple fight with subtler blues and pinks. The fabric is probably French, the design slightly reminiscent of Léger and his machine aesthetic, the colours still inspired by the Ballets Russes. Diaghilev's ballet had a profound effect on Paul Poiret who dictated fashion for a decade after World War I; it was he who encouraged artists to design textiles. Some of the most striking fabrics of all were designed by Sonia Delaunay whose work was characterized by hard geometric shapes in bold primary colours. Her fabrics were exported far and wide and became famous when film stars started using them for their wardrobes. The 'coat of many colours' she designed for Gloria Swanson is by now as legendry as Joseph's.

ABOVE
Four scent bottles in the shape of a bow-tie made by Baccarat for Guerlain of Paris. They contained a perfume called Dawamesk. It is typical of the period that a masculine design was used for an essentially feminine object. The pyjama suit or an exact copy of a man's dinner-jacket was fashionable evening wear for the flapper and this takeover of masculine fashion even found its way into toilet accessories. During the 'twenties packaging received almost as much attention as the merchandise, especially where cosmetics and perfume were concerned. Baccarat, Lalique (who designed for Coty) and Sabino are a few of the most famous glass makers who designed scent bottles, probably causing the bottle to cost as much as the scent itself.

RIGHT
Detail from a carpet in wool and chenille designed by Frank Brangwyn and made by James Templeton & Co. of Glasgow (c 1930). A pamphlet advertising the carpet says: "when an artist of the worldwide eminence of Mr Brangwyn can collaborate successfully with manufacturers, 'Art in Industry' is no longer an aspiration but a reality". Brangwyn designed furniture (for Pollard), tableware (for Doulton) and glass (for James Powell). The intention was to design good furniture for British homes at ordinary prices, "to design for the limitations of machinery, and yet produce a thing of use and beauty" ('Studio' December 1930).

20

Drop earrings in jade, onyx and diamonds by Boucheron of Paris. With the shorter hair styles of the 'twenties and 'thirties, long earrings became a very popular form of jewellery, whether made of precious stones, paste or plastic. Van Cleef and Arpels, Cartier and Boucheron were probably the three most famous jewellers of the time and catered for the mood of wealth and extravagance of the 'twenties. During the 'thirties fortunes dwindled and jewellery became severer and simpler in design. Dress-clips (designed to fit together and make a brooch), earrings and bracelets were the most fashionable accessories.

Superb platinum, onyx and diamond pendant with a real pearl. Signed by the French jeweller Lacloche. Onyx and diamonds worked together were very much the traditional jewellery of the 'twenties. During that decade great progress was

made in cutting diamonds and George Fouquet, in an article on modern jewellery in the May 1930 'Studio' says "The novelty for 1929 lies in the completely white note. But how new is this white stone jewellery and how much it differs from the old! Progress has been made in working on the diamond – pieces are composed and carried out which consists of a mixture of brilliants and brilliants cut in the form of wands, triangles, or any other form, allowing the artist to obtain from diamonds whatever effect he chooses."

ABOVE
A pen and water-colour drawing done on silk, which illustrated the mid-'twenties look. Dresses fell in a straight line from the shoulder, the bust had virtually disappeared and the waist had moved down to the hips. Hair was worn bobbed or shingled which brought earrings back into fashion. Long hair was not fashionable as it could not be concealed under cloche hats.

Hemlines varied in length from season to season: ladies' legs had after all only been on show in public since after the end of World War I and couturiers had difficulty in deciding how much leg should be shown.

RIGHT
French and English bags and shoes from the mid-'twenties. The maroon leather shoes are French. At the back is a black moiré silk evening bag by Cartier, with a decorative buddha in jade and the letter 'C' in emeralds; the green morocco bag decorated with twisted leather strips is by Finnigans of Bond Street, London. It is not known who made the other two bags. Most bags were small during the 'twenties. For day wear they were usually made of leather with chrome or plastic decorations (during the 'thirties there were elaborately designed handbags made entirely of plastic); for evening wear small embroidered or beaded bags were fashionable.

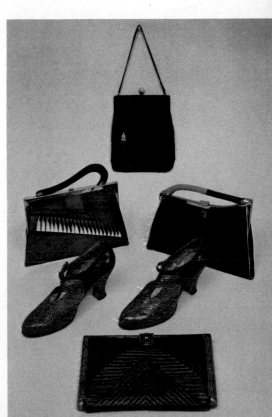

23

Dressing table and stool combined; English c 1930. By the 1920s the sanctimonious approach to the bedroom had disappeared and it was not necessary to be too serious about designing bedroom suites. There were many ingenious designs for dressing tables; some had huge circular mirrors with low shelves on either side and there were many variations of the table and stool combined. The Parisian firm of Saddier produced some of the best of these. Light fittings were often incorporated into the design, usually vertical neon tubes set into jazzy chromium fittings. The dressing table became a glorified shrine to cosmetics and fashion.

BELOW

Powder compacts, powder boxes and cigarette cases. The round glass box is by Lalique who also designed the box decorated with powder puffs for Coty (used by them until very recently). Powder was sold loose and beauty specialists recommended it be applied with fur puffs. "Do not wipe powder on, dust it on: women who 'wipe' powder on their faces use the wrong method," says an advertisement for washable, fadeless hygienic 'I'vajack puffs' in 1933. All women carried a flap-jack compact in their handbags. If you could not afford a gold compact encrusted with diamonds and rubies from Cartier, the next best thing was a compact with a jazzy enamelled design (and there were hundreds to choose from). No handbag was complete without some sort of flap-jack, which was of course changed to match the bag.

RIGHT

Three pieces of jewellery by Jean Fouquet. At the top, a ring in platinum, onyx and diamonds; in the middle, a brooch in coral, diamonds and onyx; and at the bottom, another brooch in platinum, diamonds and onyx. These pieces have a mid-'twenties feel to them, before jewellery started going ultra-modern. Jean Fouquet was one of the most original jewellery designers of the 'Deco' period; his later pieces became more geometric than those illustrated here and looks as if it is based on designs lifted straight from French cubist still-life paintings. He very much liked using precious stones combined with bakelite and plastic.

FURNITURE

LEFT
The bronze is by the Hungarian sculptor
Keleti; the wrought-iron mirror and the
commode with a design of drooping foliage
are probably of French origin; the two vases
with geometric patterns in brightly coloured
enamels are by Faure. The process of
enamelling over glass was a popular one
during the 'twenties and practised by many
of the French glass designers, but none of
them achieved the boldness of pattern or
brilliance of colour attained by Faure. Most
of his pieces are now in museums and
private collections.

RIGHT
A decorative screen designed by Frank
Brangwyn and sold by the Rowley Gallery,
London. Many artists designed decorative
panels and screens during the 'twenties and
'thirties though it is rare to find one in inlaid
wood. Lacquer work came back into fashion
and was more usual for this type of
decoration. There were several artists who
specialized in this work; perhaps the best
known was Jean Dunand whose most
famous screen was one 22 feet high and
27 feet across designed for the smoking-room
of the transatlantic liner 'Normandie'. Eileen
Gray, an English designer working in Paris,
was another artist whose lacquer screens
were superbly made and beautifully
designed.

RIGHT
Table by Emile-Jacques Ruhlmann especially
designed for the Yardley premises in Old
Bond Street. The table is in Macassar ebony
and brass bound at the foot. Ruhlmann in
conjunction with Reco Capey designed a
complete scheme for Yardleys in the early
'thirties at the very end of his life. He died in
1933 after a lifetime's reputation as one of the
greatest of French decorators. He was only
interested in designing for the richest
collectors and his furniture made no
concessions to the growing demand for
artist-designed pieces at commercial prices.
He used the rarest woods and infinite work
and craftsmanship went into every piece. His
'Pavillon d'un Collectionneur' was one of
the highlights of the 1925 Paris Exhibition.

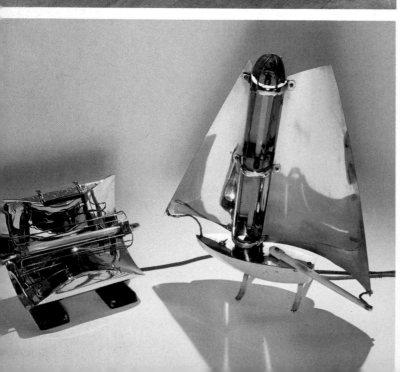

TOP LEFT
Blonde wood bureau and drawers with brass handles and panels of antelope skin; on gilded base with scroll-like decoration. The use of antelope skin has a touch of surrealism about it, though it is not as pronounced as Schiaparelli's sofa in the shape of lips or her hat in the shape of a shoe. It is difficult to suggest any maker for this piece of furniture. Furniture varied greatly in order to suit the whim of a particular decorator or client, and no material was considered too impractical. There were some favourites (sharkskin, lacquer, glass or aluminium, for instance), but every designer fought for originality of style, and was eager to find new and untried materials to work in.

LEFT
English peach mirror glass table by James Clark Ltd c. 1935. White and coloured mirror glass and mirror furniture was very fashionable during the 'thirties. With improved manufacturing techniques glass became more flexible and more varied. There were mirror glass cocktail cabinets, desks and clocks and the English designer Oliver Hill even designed a dangerous sounding glass chaise longue supported by four glass balls, (though this was intended primarily for exhibition purposes). Oliver Hill was also responsible in collaboration with Lady Mount Temple for a spectacular bathroom in which walls, ceiling and all fitments were grey mirror glass, and the bath and basin lined in gold mosaic.

FAR LEFT
Two 1930s electric fires, one in the shape of a sailing-boat, the sails acting both as reflectors and heat conductors; the other a modernist design in polished chrome. There were several variations on the sailing-boat fire, one of the commonest being a butterfly electric fire. As with lighters and radios, designers could give free reign to their

fantasies when it came to modern household equipment for which there was no real precedent. It was a refreshing aspect of design between the wars that a light-hearted joke was perfectly acceptable if the finished object was practical and well thought out.

BELOW LEFT
Dressing table, stool and mirror by the American designer Paul Frankl, who wrote in his work 'Form and Reform' published in 1930: "Ornament = crime. Here is the axiom of extreme modernism." American interior design did not begin to go modern until 1930 or slightly before. There were plenty of American interior decorators during the 1920s but more often than not they tried to capture a European feel in interiors they designed. An all Spanish, or all Italianate, or all French Empire room was what they were after more than the all modern look. American Modernism did not really catch on till the 'thirties.

LEFT
The bronze and ivory figure of a lady with two greyhounds is by Chiparus. The delicate 1920s lady's writing desk has a matt crackled polish overlaid with stylized painted flower and fruit decoration. The decoration is typically French, probably of the period between 1918 and 1925. It is reminiscent of the work of Paul Follot or André Mare, both of whom used flower and fruit in characteristically Art Deco designs, and it might perhaps come from the workshops of one of the big stores in Paris where these designers worked. Follot was responsible for the workshop at the Bon Marché, and Mare in conjunction with Sue founded the Compagnie des Arts Français as early as 1919.

ABOVE
Display cabinet in dark wood with ivory inlay by Paul Follot. This cabinet was shown at the 1925 Paris Exhibition. The flower and leaf decoration running down the central dividing strip is typical of this designer who catered for enlightened middle-brow taste. His furniture, whilst incorporating Art Deco design, stuck to fairly traditional shapes and ideas. This was partly due to the fact that he had to design with the general public in mind, as from 1923 onwards he was head of the decorating department at one of the largest Paris department stores, Bon Marché.

ABOVE RIGHT
Mirror and cabinet by Carlo Bugatti. Not very much is known about Bugatti – he lived through both the Art Nouveau and Art Deco periods and exhibited at the famous Turin Exhibition in 1902. His style was completely individual, with a strong oriental influence. His furniture tends to be impractical (for example his huge uncomfortable chairs), but every piece displays a superb sense of craftsmanship. The cabinet above is beautifully inlaid with metal and brass, the mirror is leather painted with a floral design. Bugatti's designs bridge the gap between Art Nouveau and Art Deco, between romanticism to geometry. The bronze and ivory figure on the cabinet is by Chiparus.

RIGHT
French side-cupboard with Chiparus bronze and ivory figure of a dancing lady and above that a pair of wall bracket lights by René Lalique. Although he was over 60 years old at the beginning of the 1920s, Lalique's output was enormous and he was the sole designer of the glassware produced by the firm. His son helped him with the economic and productional aspects of the business and the work exhibited by the firm at the Paris International Exhibition of 1925 brought world-wide recognition. Lalique experimented in the field of illuminated glass and design pieces that were meant primarily as decorative ornaments rather than sources of light.

Weighing-machine, chair and table at Radio City Music Hall, New York; the chair and table are by Deskey. This remarkable "height weight metre" is shaped like a skyscraper – a typical piece of 1930s American 'modernism' Paul Frankl, who was famous for his skyscraper bookcases and display cabinets, said of the American skyscraper: "We had our skyscrapers and at that very date (1925) they had been developed to such an extent that, if it had been possible to have sent an entire building abroad, it would have been a more vital contribution in the field of modern art than all the things done in Europe added together."

Dining table by René Lalique made in c1931. Only a few of these tables were made – the top is one thick sheet of opalescent glass, supported by four glass columns on a solid glass base, the whole held together by a framework of chromium-plated metal. Lalique's output was so vast and varied that it would have been possible to acquire a complete dinner service made by the firm including menu holders and candelabra. Lighting could be from one of his beautiful decorative lamps or glass wall brackets. Only food and cutlery might upset the scheme.

INTERIOR DESIGN

PREVIOUS PAGE
I.S. Chanin's bathroom in the executive suite of the Chanin building on Lexington Avenue and 42nd street, New York. The building was completed in 1929. The interior decoration was by Jacques Delamarre under the supervision of I.S. Chanin (head of the Chanin Construction Company Inc.). This bathroom in the sky, on the 52nd floor of the skyscraper block, is decorated with cream and gold tiles; the small frieze of ceramic bird tiles above the bath conceals a ventilating duct. The shower and basin taps, the rims of the heavy engraved glass shower doors and the sun burst pattern above these doors are all gold-plated. A splendid example of the extravagance and splendour of American 'Modernism'.

BELOW
A corner of Roxy's private suite in Radio City Music Hall, with furniture and lighting by Donald Deskey. S. L. Rothafel, known better, or almost exclusively as Roxy, was the genius behind this fantastic music hall, theatre and cinema combined with its 36 precision dancing Rockettes, its vast stage and incredible foyers and lounges fitted with carpets, wallpapers, furniture, murals, chandeliers, bronzework and statuary, all executed by artists of the modern school. Leading American artists were commissioned to lend their talents to the decorative scheme. The most modern materials were used wherever possible: aluminium, cork, bakelite and formica; pyroxalin-coated fabric; structural mirrors and glass walls; honeyskin, tweed, pigskin and patent-leather upholstery and furniture of chrome-plated steel and tube aluminium.

RIGHT
A detail of the entrance hall to the Daily Express Building, Fleet Street, London (1931). The architect responsible for designing the entrance hall was Robert Atkinson. Serge Chermayeff, writing in the 'Architectural Review' for July 1932, describes it as "a mass of fibrous plaster, gilded and silvered in the tinsel manner, suggesting a provincial picture palace". John Betjeman, writing 40 years later calls it "a fabulous Art Deco entrance hall, with wonderful rippling confections of metal". On the exterior of the building black strips of glass set in chromium curve around the corner on which it stands, giving a marvellous effect of modernism and streamlining.

LEFT
Part of the foyer at the Savoy Theatre, London, showing the ceiling, a decorative urn, and one of the radiator grilles designed by Basil Ionides, who redecorated the theatre in 1929. This designer was responsible for some of the best interior design in London during the 'twenties and early 'thirties, including work at the Savoy Hotel, Claridge's and Swan and Edgar's. In an article on Interior Design in 'Studio' Magazine for May 1929, Ionides wrote: "Simplicity is of course the note to be aimed at today, and also good colours. The day of the elaborate plaster ceiling is gone and its place is taken by simple stepping or coffering."

RIGHT
Replicas of Edgar Brandt's wrought-iron and bronze decorative panels. The originals were made in 1922 or 1923; the replicas were made to decorate the interiors of the lifts at Selfridge's when the Oxford Street store was rebuilt in the 'twenties. Recently the lifts were modernized and the panels given to various museums in England. One is constantly amazed how Brandt could hammer and coax iron into such delicate shapes, full of expression and movement. However intricate his work, whether it be a radiator grille, a lamp, a decorative panel, or a piece of furniture, it always achieves a superb balance between practicability and decoration.

RIGHT
A recently converted 1930s style bedroom. Although not authentic in every detail, the curving mirror strips, the tubular steel and plate glass of the shelves behind the bed, the furniture, the objects and the light fittings by Lalique give a distinct feeling of the 'thirties to the room. There has been a great revival of interest in design between the wars brought about by important exhibitions such as 'Les Années '25' at the Musée de l'Art Moderne in Paris in 1966 and the Minneapolis exhibition in 1970. It has affected and inspired designers in the early 1970s most noticeably in the graphic arts, with lettering and art-work of the 'twenties and 'thirties appearing frequently in advertising features and on posters.

LEFT
Anteroom to Claridge's ballroom, Brook Street, London. Claridge's was re-decorated in 1929 under the supervision of Basil Ionides, and became a showcase for the work of some of the best English designers and interior decorators; the new ballroom was designed by Oswald P. Milne with a series of decorative panels by George Sheringham; the carpets were by Marion Dorn. The greatest effort has been made to preserve this extravagent decoration – when stair carpets wear out new ones are woven to the old design. The Causerie, the main lobby, the restaurant, the ballroom, the bedrooms and the bathrooms all retain the splendour of the 'twenties as far as possible.

BELOW LEFT
Elevator doors in the lobby of the First National City Trust Co., originally the City Bank Farmers Trust Co. in the Wall Street district of New York. The building was put up in 1931. The elevator doors are of monel, a mixture of nickel and brass. It was high speed elevators (together with American steel-frame construction) that made skyscrapers possible, and one of the most important features in determining the success of an office building was the speed, efficiency and comfort of the elevators. Everything was done to make elevator doors and elevator cars as eye-catching and as attractive as possible.

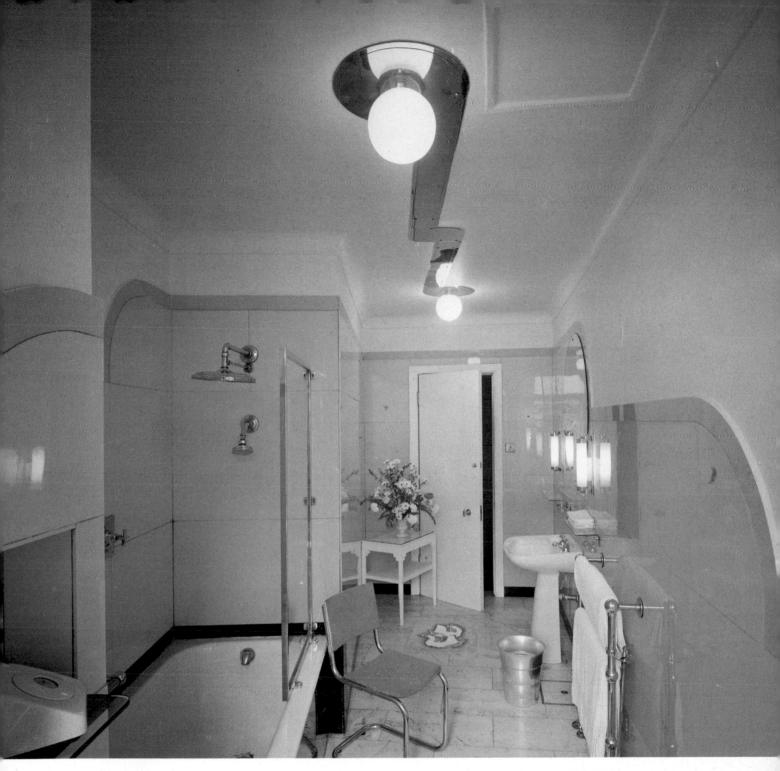

LEFT
Superb wrought-iron mirror by Edgar Brandt. The marble-topped console table is also by Brandt; the two lamps have 'Pâte de verre' shades by Argy-Rousseau. 'Pâte de verre' was a very thick, almost opaque glass; it was used to make vases and ornaments and was particularly effective when used for lampshades, assuming a jewel-like effect when light shone through it. 'Pâte de verre' was a process whereby finished glass was ground into powder, mixed with liquid (usually water) and then cooked in a mould. It was used by a variety of glass designers, notably Argy Rousseau, Décorchemont and Lalique.

ABOVE
A bathroom at Claridge's (c 1930) decorated with the latest glass and chromium fittings; the floor is white speckled marble. It was a comparatively new idea to 'design' a bathroom. Decorators went mad; for instance, Armand-Albert Rateau designed a bathroom for Jeanne Lanvin in which the bath and washbasin were in Siennese yellow marble and the fittings were decorated with butterflies, acanthus leaves, palms and pheasants. But, generally speaking, with improved sanitary fittings, a wide selection of decorative tiles, coloured opaque glass (nitaline) and rubber flooring with jazzy designs, bathrooms could be elegant without too much expense.

FOLLOWING PAGES
The women's lounge on the first mezzanine at Radio City Music Hall, New York. The painted wall decorations are by Yasuo Kuniyoshi, who was born in Japan in 1893, came to America as a young boy and lived and worked there. The 31 smoking-rooms and lounges in Radio City Music Hall are sumptuously decorated and fitted out in various 'modern' styles. Various suitable themes are used: for instance, 'Men Without Women' is the subject of a large abstract mural in the basement men's smoking-room, whilst the women's smoking room on the same floor has a series of murals in white on white parchment depicting 'A History of Cosmetics'.

LEFT

A French bronze and ivory figure of a girl dancing and holding a silver ball, signed "Lip". A chryselephantine sculpture (sculpture in ivory and precious metals) was one of the most popular ornaments in a 'modern' drawing room of the 'twenties and 'thirties. Either they were high camp dancing girls in extraordinary poses with amazing hairstyles or headgear; or the more conventional neo-classical figures. The base was usually elegantly shaped in different coloured marbles or in onyx. These figures are now valuable collectors' items and fetch high prices.

RIGHT

Two pieces from the "Wienerwerkstaette" by Hagenauer (c1925); one is a mirror with pewter frame, the other (reflected in the mirror) a free-standing group in polished chrome and ebony. The Vienna workshops were founded in 1903 by Professor Josef Hoffmann, the famous Austrian architect, and this association of artists, designers and craftsmen came to gain great significance. There was hardly a field in which its influence was not felt; interior decorating, furniture, ceramics, enamel, crystal and silver, the graphic arts and fabrics. Gustav Klint, Egon Schiele and Oskar Kokoschka were among the artists who worked for the Werkstaette for a while.

RIGHT

Philips radio with Chinese lacquer work design. Wireless broadcasting was still in its infancy during the 'twenties. When Dame Nellie Melba made her first broadcast in 1920 from Chelmsford she was said to be "the first great operatic celebrity to risk the possible distortion of her voice over the wireless". Radios came in all shapes and sizes, some were outrageously 'modernist', others were designed to tone in with the more conservative backgrounds. The radio illustrated here falls into the second category. Apart from the mere fact of its being a radio, it is the geometric design of the speaker cutting into the decoration that makes it a modern piece of furniture.

LEFT
The work of two of the finest European craftsmen is seen together in this illustration. Four bronze and ivory figures by Chiparus are displayed on a console table in wrought iron with a marble top designed by Edgar Brandt. Brandt's ironwork attracted much attention at the 1925 Paris Exhibition and his designs in ironwork were compared to jewellery. Little is known about Chiparus except that he was Rumanian and worked in Paris. He exhibited at the Salon des Artistes Français from 1914 to 1928. The dancer depicted in the third figure from the left is Nijinsky.

RIGHT
Silver fruit bowl designed by the Danish silversmith Georg Jensen (1866–1935). Although this actual piece was made only a few years ago, it is an exact copy of a piece designed by Jensen. This great craftsman died in 1935 and an obituary in the January 1936 'Studio' says: "It is safe to say that no other silversmith in the present or any other age exercised a more potent and profound influence on contemporary design in his own particular field than this sincere and single-hearted genius." Jensen's designs relied on stark simplicity for effect and such embellishment as he used was always "restrained, logical and inevitable".

BELOW LEFT
Two-handled silver cup and cover designed by R M Y Gleadhowe, made by H G Murphy and engraved by G T Friends (1938). This was a gift to the National Council of Physical Fitness from the Worshipful Company of Goldsmiths. Gleadhowe was Art Master at Winchester College, Slade Professor at Oxford, and died whilst working at the Admiralty during the war. His work was marked by delicate and detailed pictorial engraving, in this case a series of panels which in true 'thirties tradition idolize sport and the outdoor life. His output of work was small, but every piece he made is highly individual in style and carefully thought out to the last detail.

RIGHT
A moulded car-mascot by René Lalique, in which the prancing horses are the embodiment of speed – one of the obsessions of the 'twenties and 'thirties. The Italian futurist poet, Marinetti, says: "Speed is our god; the new canon of beauty, a racing car is more beautiful than the victory of Samothrace." 'Studio' magazine for February 1931 has an article on Lalique's car mascots, and says: "A car figurehead is essentially an item of decor, as much so as a glittering ornament in a lady's hat." The glass in these mascots was plain white but any colour effect could be achieved as an interchangeable light filter could be placed over the bulb that lit the mascot.

British silver partly owes its high standard of workmanship to the interest and patronage of the Worshipful Company of Goldsmiths (where every piece of English silver or silver imported into England goes to be hallmarked). The company encouraged students at art schools and designers in factories to design practical things like tea-sets and cutlery, whilst commissioning artist-craftsmen and small workshops to make exhibition pieces for propaganda purposes at home and abroad. In the illustration the four round boxes are by H G Murphy (all c1930). Of the box with three red balls on top the one-time clerk of the company of goldsmiths writes: "Murphy trying to outdo the Germans in art and decoration and going modern". The little bowl with niello decoration is by Bernard Cuzner (1933), and the cigarette box by C J Shiner.

TOP LEFT
Rectangular pewter tobacco box with stepped lid and formalized flower pattern engraved on sides, designed by A E Poulter (who was a drawing instructor at Kingston Art School) and made by A R Emerson; dating from 1935. Pewter had been very much used by Art Nouveau metalwork designers but seems to have been unfashionable after that period. Although Liberty still advertised artist designed pewter in 'Studio' magazines of the 'twenties and 'thirties, many of the designs dated from around the turn of the century and the later designs are of little interest. It is unusual to find a really successful 'modern' piece like that illustrated here.

TOP RIGHT
Flask and stopper by Maurice Marinot made in 1929. Green glass with black enclosures, acid-etched. Marinot (1882–1960) started life as a painter but gave this up and decided to express his "visions of light and colour" in glass. He was fascinated by strange shapes and textures and was an innovator inasmuch as he introduced bubbles and bulges with planned precision such as the ordinary glass manufacturer would take the greatest pains to eliminate from the finished product. In the 26 years he spent making glass he produced only 2,500 pieces. One of the finest collections of Marinot glass is that given to the Victoria and Albert Museum in 1964 by Florence Marinot.

FAR LEFT
Glass dish on a decorative wrought-iron base, hand-painted on the underside of the glass and signed Quenvit. This artist either painted or enamelled his designs on to glass, using vivid floral patterns with a distinctly geometric feel: it is the decoration rather than the shape of the glass which gives the piece a period style. Following the tradition of earlier French glass designers some of Quenvit's pieces incorporate metalwork. Being hand-painted, his glass is ornamental rather than practical, and was intended for interior decoration first and foremost.

LEFT
Decorative glass vase framed in wrought iron; the glass is by Daum of Nancy, the metal work by Majorelle. Both of these were well known names during the Art Nouveau period as well as the Art Deco period. It is interesting to note the complete change in style that their work underwent. This is particularly noticeable in Majorelle's case. Here his work is angular and geometric. During the Art Nouveau period, however, he designed furniture with the most luxuriant whiplash decorations based on exotic plant motifs. Speckled coloured glass was used by many of the French glass makers at this period, especially Daum and Muller Frères of Luneville.

French clock by Jean Trenchant in polished steel on a marble base. This is a radically modern design for a clock where the strongest effect is achieved by exercising the severest economy of design. Le Corbusier and Walter Gropius would have approved. Clocks were made of wood, chromium, silver, glass or marble; of any material or design that would complement a modern interior. The obsession with total design meant that every object had to fit into a scheme and as most rooms had a clock, an endless variety was designed, from the most expensive silver and ivory clock decorated with amber, coloured plastic and diamonds by Cartier, to the simplest mirror-glass electric wall-clock by Smiths.

POTTERY AND PORCELAIN

PREVIOUS PAGE
A collection of porcelain ladies by Doulton, Royal Dux and others. On the top shelf from left to right: the sailor girl is by Royal Dux of Bavaria; Clotilde, the Lido Lady and Columbine by the English firm of Doulton. The bottom shelf contains another Doulton figurine called "Scotties", a pair of sitting ladies (origin unknown) and a pair of amazingly stylized scent bottles (probably German). The green bases contain the perfume and the heads are in fact stoppers to which glass dip-sticks are attached. Figurines of ladies were immensely popular and most of the famous porcelain manufacturers had some in their catalogue.

LEFT
Hand-painted porcelain figure of a dancing pair by Clarice Cliff in her 'Bizarre' series. She is supposed to have designed five different dancing pairs in all. One cannot tell what dance this couple is doing, possibly the tango, which, with the Charleston was all the rage. Tango also lent its name to a burnt orange colour now very much associated with the 'twenties. The ball gown

and tails suggest a formal evening occasion rather than an afternoon frittered away at a rango-tea or 'thé dansant'.

BELOW
English bone china coffee set, with silver lustre and pale green design of abstract foliage; produced by A E Gray & Co, Tunstall, Staffs, designed by Susie Cooper and sold by Peter Jones of London. The set is illustrated in the 'Studio Yearbook of Decorative Art' for 1929, where in an article on pottery and glassware it says, "All is not yet well between the artist and the machine, but everything points to the fact that the people are weary of ugliness and will only be satisfied with worthy things worthily made for a worthy purpose." A tremendous effort was made to 'industrialize' the arts and crafts, and as far as ceramics were concerned, to link up the work of the studio potter with industry.

BELOW RIGHT
A group of Belgian ceramic pieces made by Keramis and Boch La Louvière. Most of the pottery by these two firms seems to have a grey-white crackled surface broken by

vividly coloured geometric floral designs in shiny enamelled glazes. Studio pottery was popular in Europe and much space was devoted to ceramics in the 1925 Paris Exhibition. The most interesting (and today valuable) pieces were signed by the artists, and manufacturers encouraged well-known painters to design for them. Bonnard, Derain, Matisse and Vlaminck are among those who designed pottery in France.

RIGHT
Three jazz-musicians made for the Parisian porcelain firm of Robj (c1930). Robj sold decorative figures of all sorts; many of them were useful household objects in disguise. For instance in a set of licqueur bottles, one was a policeman, another a monk; there was a three-piece licqueur set consisting of golfing figures; there was a porcelain lamp in the shape of a cowboy. Most of the figures were slightly comical and cartoon-like. These 'bibelots' were tremendously popular and are now much collected. As the Robj advertisement ran in the 'twenties: 'Les bibelots signés Robj sont le complément de tout intérieur élégant.'

ABOVE
A "Tea for Two" set designed by Clarice Cliff (c1929), one of the most imaginative English designers of tableware of the late 'twenties and 'thirties. Clarice Cliff (1900–1970) first worked at the Burslem firm of A J Wilkinson as an apprentice and was later made Art Director. She produced an astonishing variety of brightly coloured designs, some of them conventional, like her well-known 'crocus pattern', others (in the 'Bizarre' and 'Fantasque' series particularly) more adventurous and abstract. Her table-sets were immensely popular, and were often featured in fashion magazines of the period. Her work was sold in great quantities in Great Britain and was also exported to Australia and New Zealand amongst other countries.

LEFT
A group of plates and vases designed by Charlotte Rhead for Crown Ducal Potteries, probably dating from the mid-'thirties. Charlotte Rhead's work is easily recognizable, with stylized flower and leaf patterns in gay colours, rather reminiscent of floral chintzes, The colours of the designs are painted over an underglazed and contained within the raised outlines of the pattern. This method of obtaining icing-sugar-like outline decoration was known as 'tubeline decoration', and was a very expensive process demanding considerable skill. Most pieces are signed "C Rhead", and a few are signed in full. The plywood trolley on which the pieces are displayed is by Heal's.

A group of salt-glaze ceramic vases decorated by various artists for Royal Doulton (c. 1920–1935). Salt-glaze ceramics had their day in the Victorian era, but Doulton's Lambeth and Burslem potteries continued to produce studio-designed pieces until the Lambeth pottery finally closed in 1957. As with most later Doulton pieces, the vases in this illustration retain basically Victorian shapes, but they are remarkable for their unusual colouring and decoration. Vera Huggins, Eliza Simmance and Bessie Newbury were three of the most distinctive Doulton studio designers of the 'twenties. There was also work by outside artists including Frank Brangwyn and Reco Capey, the Professor of Design at the Royal College of Art.

Wall plate by Carter, Stabler, Adams Ltd, Poole Pottery, Dorset; with an impressed mark dating from about 1925. The Poole pottery (still in existence today) was an amalgamation of a tile-making firm and a studio of artists including John Adams, Truda Adams, Harold & Phoebe Stabler and Truda Carter. It is difficult to distinguish between the work of these artists; they all painted in a similar style. But the work of the pottery was very distinctive, usually with decorative stylized birds and flowers hand-painted in delicate pastel colours over a powdered grey glaze. Many pieces by the firm are illustrated in the 'Studio' Decorative Yearbooks.

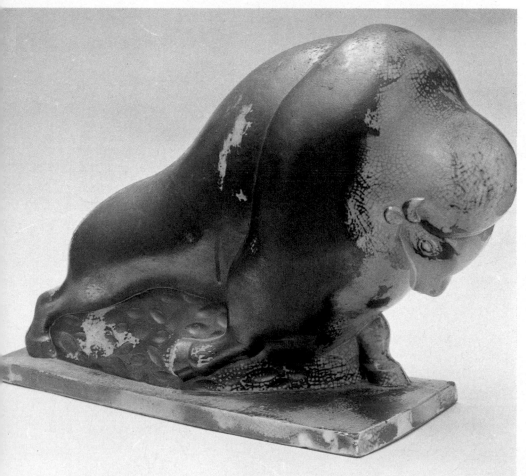

Porcelain bison made for Primavera. Primavera was the name of the Art Studio of the Grands Magasins du Printemps in Paris. The studio was established by the Printemps in September 1912 for the creation of decorative art models. In the first year they produced 813 models. An advertisement in the 1928 'Studio' decorative art yearbook goes on to say: "It has developed progressively during the last fifteen years and has now reached the figure of 13,750 models. The creations of the Primavera Studio are produced by its ceramique factory at Sainte Radegonde, near Tours, and by its cabinet works at Montreuil-sous-bois to which are attached workshops for bronzes, sculpture, iron work and decoration in lacquer."

ADVERTISING
AND
PRINTING

PREVIOUS PAGE
Frontispiece illustration by John Austen to Manon Lescaut, published by Geoffrey Bles in 1928 in an edition limited to 500 copies. John Austen was remarkable for his superb colouring and beautiful line drawing which owes something to the Beardsley tradition. Herbert Grimsditch, in an article in 'Studio' (August 1924), entitled "Mr John Austen and the Art of the Book", says: "Mr Austen makes no claim to illustrate a book in the realistic sense; he does not attempt to represent in line what the word itself should have conveyed to the thoughtful mind, but, taking the book as a book, he decorates it with drawings into which he infuses the spirit of the text".

BELOW
Prometheus, a glazed pottery figure made by Ashtead potteries for Hope's Heating & Lighting Ltd from a design by Percy Metcalfe. It was used by Hope's to advertise the firm. The 'Studio' Yearbook for 1929 says of Ashtead: "The work of the Ashtead Potteries is one of the most remarkable developments of Industrial Art . . . a band of disabled ex-soldiers, broken and worn by years of pain . . . . were set to work with strange tools, upon new and strange fabric. They had no previous training, no apparent predilection for this art or that, but were set down in the potter's studio to learn its technique. Out of a scheme for providing the opportunities to make a livelihood has grown an industry that has already left an indelible mark in matters of sound pottery, good design, real utility, and the satisfying of good taste at small cost."

RIGHT
A random selection of 'twenties and 'thirties song covers. In the 'twenties and particularly the 'thirties with Hollywood musicals in their prime, musical comedy had its heyday. In America tunes by Cole Porter, Jerome Kern, Gershwin, Arlen, Benin, Rogers and Hart filled the air. In England Noel Coward and Ivor Novello enjoyed immense popularity. Amazing Deco sets were built for what is already known as 'the golden age of Hollywood musicals' and Busby Berkeley invented fantastic geometric effects on the screen with his chorus girl routines. Some of all this fantasy was carried over into the colour and design of song covers. There was an enormous market for song albums and sheet music; television had not yet managed to kill live entertainment at home.

BELOW
A vase by Bernardaud & Co of Limoges, made especially for the French furrier 'A La Reine d'Angleterre'. The vase was presumably given away by the firm as an advertisement. Elegant ladies draped in furs float around the vase suspended on clouds. It is not quite clear what furs they are wearing, but the great vogue of the 1920s was for fox, especially for silver fox, though fur of every kind was popular. As real fur was prohibitively expensive substitutes and imitations began to appear. According to James Laver in 'Taste and Fashion' fur was in such great demand that in the late 'twenties there was hardly any fur-bearing animal which was not made to contribute to feminine attire.

PROMETHEUS

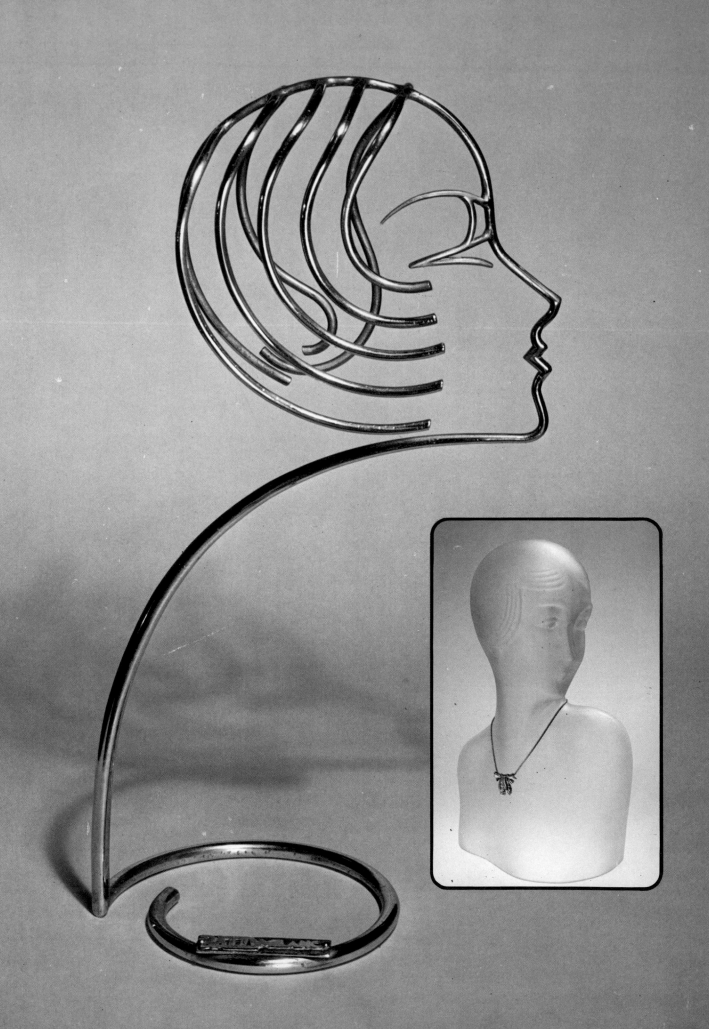

LEFT

Polished chromium hat stand made for the Italian firm of Bazzi in Milan. A supremely simple, supremely elegant design that captures the look and feel of the 'twenties, partly with the use of chromium (which became increasingly popular for all sorts of furniture and fittings), and again with the unmistakably 'twenties boy-girl profile. The shingled hair closely followed the line of the head and made it possible to wear cloche hats which dominated the fashion world from about 1925 to 1930.

Blue ice-glass head, probably used to display hats in a milliner's window: what in the 'twenties was just a shop fitting has today earned itself a place as a minor work of art, and in retrospect looks like a source of pop-art. Ice-glass was used for lamps, lampshades, scent bottles, vases; plates and many other practical and decorative pieces. It came in a great variety of colours and was a cheaper version of the beautiful opalescent glass made famous by Lalique. Marcel waves, as worn by this model, were invented in 1906 by the Parisian hair stylist, Marcel, and became very popular when ladies cropped their hair during the 'twenties, particularly in the late 'twenties when ladies wanted a change from the very severe hairstyles that fashion dictated in the earlier part of the decade.

ABOVE

John Player & Son cigarette cards: a selection from a set of fifty entitled "Straight Line Caricatures" designed by Alick P F Ritchie, and issued in 1926. They are cubist portraits of famous people. Most tobacco firms issued cigarette cards and subjects ranged from 'Pugilists in Action' to 'Our Puppies'. Many sets were devoted to the cinema and film stars. In 'Cigarette Cards and how to collect them' I O Evans says "Most people feel a need, in this mechanical civilization, of some spare-time activity which they can pursue for its own sake. To this end cigarette card collecting has much to recommend it."

RIGHT

Poster designed by E S McKnight Kauffer for Eastman & Son (1922). In the 1924 special poster number of the 'Studio' McKnight Kauffer is described as designing excellent posters "conceived in the modern decorative manner". During the 'twenties posters became bolder and simpler. Their message had to be delivered far more quickly than in Toulouse Lautrec's day. Then the passer-by had time to read and appreciate a poster, but the flapper speeding past at 25 miles per hour had less time to spare. The growing importance of mass-production made publicity vital: a lot of money was spent on poster art

Fabrics ... that color the lives of women

THE NAME ABERFOYLE on the ends of the board around which the material is rolled assures quality. ABERFOYLE Fabrics are fully guaranteed as to quality and fast color. They are dyed in the yarn, then each piece is thoroughly laundered before leaving the mill.

THERE is a fascination for some women in pale pinks and yellows. Through the lives of others may be traced a thread of blue. Color can change a sleeping brunette into a vivacious creature—and color acts like magic on a blonde.

By the shades and tones of their frocks and dresses, women paint their types—just as an artist puts himself into each canvas.

A careful choice between a pale rose voile and a blue and white tissue—the selection of a fabric with a small flowered design rather than a gaily plaided one—then the actual style and making of the frock ... in these every artist-woman revels.

Among Aberfoyle Fabrics there are materials in many shades and even more designs. In the shops one sees Aberfoyle Fabrics in a palette-ful of shades ... shades like a color chart from which each woman chooses. The designs are appropriate for every occasion—French designs for summer—bold designs for sport. There's not a colorful piece of Aberfoyle Fabrics but what may be washed as often as you please—washed with soap and water. Aberfoyle Fabrics are on display in shops throughout the country and are distributed to wholesalers by Galey & Lord, Inc., New York City.

Aberfoyle Fabrics

LEFT
Advertisement in the April 1928 issue of 'McCall's', designed by Helen Dryden. 'McCall's' carried some of the most stylish advertisements of the Deco period and back numbers of the magazine reveal some of the the best American graphic design.

It was not only the fashion houses that were design conscious when it came to advertising. Essex cakes, Campbell's soup, Wesson oil or Ipana toothpaste were just a few of the firms whose advertisements seem worth singling out. But in general American poster design before the 'thirties was more traditional than the advertisement for Aberfoyle fabrics illustrated here.

BELOW
A poster advertising Hyde Park, London, designed by Jean Dupas, signed and dated 1930; the caption is a quotation from Samuel Pepys's diaries. This poster was commissioned by the London Underground, and is one of many designed for the railways by famous artists. Martin Battersby refers to Dupas as "a major artist active in the 'twenties". Poster art was treated very seriously between the wars, and a special autumn number of the 'Studio' in 1924 entitled "Posters and their Designers" begins with the words: "This is the day of the poster ... some of the best brains in the business world of today are concentrated on the possibilities of the poster as a means for advancing trade".

"Thence to Hyde Park, where much good company, and many fine Ladies"

ARCHITECTURE

PREVIOUS PAGE
The BBC building in Portland Place, London, designed by Lt-Col. G Val Mayer with sculptural decorations by Eric Gill and Vernon Hill. It was completed in 1932 and was described in the 'Architectural Review' (August 1932) as parting the road "like a battleship floating towards the observer". The building, referred to as the New Tower of London, excited much criticism for being excessively modern. The 'Architectural Review' said: "The finished building represents the outcome of a struggle between moribund traditionalism and inventive modernism . . . in this case, fortunately, the struggle ended in a victory which largely favoured the modernists."

BELOW
Decorative panels above the main entrance to the 'RCA' Building, Rockefeller Plaza, New York. 'Wisdom' as conceived by the sculptor Lee Lawrie, looks down from the clouds over the central section of the main entrance to the building. Above the flanking sections are figures representing 'light' and 'sound'. The effectiveness of the sculptured treatment is enhanced by the use of polychrome by Leon V Solon, and by the cast glass wall below. The wall, 55 feet long and 15 feet high is moulded in high relief. It is constructed of uniform blocks of glass bonded in vinelite and reinforced by steel rods. The glass was made by the Steuben glass works.

RIGHT
Architectural drawing for a factory in Hammersmith dated 1930. The design is typical of that of many factories built during the early 'thirties: long, low buildings with plenty of glass and an impressive central doorway. Many such buildings are still standing, the most impressive of which is probably the Hoover building at Perivale, just outside London. The buildings and their interior decoration were considered important enough for the 'Architectural Review' to devote considerable space and often whole numbers to factory architecture. As the 'twenties and 'thirties were very design conscious, money spent on designing factories was considered a good investment as they could win prestige and publicity from business clients as well as the general public.

BELOW RIGHT
One of three plaques that decorate the exterior of Radio City Music Hall. The three circular plaques of metal and enamel were designed by Hildreth Meiers and executed by Oscar B Bach. The plaque illustrated here represents the spirit of Drama; the other two represent Song and Dance. The music hall was opened on 27 December 1932; it has a seating capacity of 6,200 and its aim (as the current publicity handout informs us) was "to achieve a complete decorative scheme that is an example of sane modern design, as differentiated from modernistic design that merely takes as a starting point deviation from an established form".

30 ROCKEFELLER PLAZA

62

Two views of the Hoover factory on the A40 at Perivale just outside London, built by Wallis, Gilbert & Partners in 1932. Nicholas Pevsner describes it as "perhaps the most offensive of the modernistic atrocities along this road of typical by-pass factories". To the Art Deco enthusiast the effect of streamlining, the brilliant fan-shaped windows going round corners, the linear use of strong colours contrasting with the white of the building, all represent the best in British factory architecture of the period. The decoration above the main entrance of the Hoover building is particularly splendid and has been the subject of much comment. Writers have seen exotic influences of all sorts in the design. Bevis Hillier probably comes closest in his 'World of Art Deco' when he says: "Ballet Russe, Aztec or Egyptian? Even if one could speak to the architect, he might not be able to give an answer." All these influences were present in decorative design at some stage, and designers or architects translated an idea or conglomeration of ideas to fit the modern idiom. Certainly the influence of Le Corbusier and his 'white dream' are felt in factory architecture of the period. "All houses should be white by law" pleaded Le Corbusier; "This cleanliness shows objects in their absolute veracity and implies the obligation of absolute purity." Other factories worth looking at near London are the Firestone Building on the Old London Airport road and the Coty building opposite.

ABOVE
The 1,046 ft Chrysler building is the embodiment of American Deco, particularly the multi-arched dome that tops the structure. The building is faced in Nirosta metal chosen by Walter P Chrysler because it had an "attractive dignified colour similar to platinum". When it was completed in 1930 an article appeared in 'the American Architect' about the designer, William van Alen, who was sometimes known as "the Ziegfield of his profession": it sums up contemporary reaction to the style. "Do you or don't you? That is the question. Some do. Some don't. Some think it's a freak; some think it's a stunt. A few think it is positively ugly; others consider it a great feat, a masterpiece, a 'tour de force'."

ABOVE RIGHT
The Empire State Building, New York, built by Shreve, Lamb and Harmon in 1930. American skyscraper architecture during the 'twenties and 'thirties delighted and surprised the world – it was America's contribution to Art Deco. Many articles have been written about Aztec influences and the pyramid-like shape of skyscrapers. In fact the shape of skyscrapers during the 'twenties and 'thirties was governed principally by the zoning laws of 1916 which produced the set-back arrangement because it was no longer permissible to build towers that rose in a solid mass to enormous heights. The higher a building rose, the narrower the tower had to be in relation to the total ground space occupied by the building, in order to avoid claustrophobic overcrowding and allow in as much light and air as possible at the top of the building.

RIGHT
570 Lexington Avenue, New York; an example of a 1930s modernist skyscraper. This one was built in 1931 by the architects

Cross and Cross, whose skyscraper architecture has changed and progressed since then and still continues to enhance the New York skyline. Arnold Lehmann, in 'The Metropolitan Museum of Art Bulletin' (April 1971), writes of skyscrapers of the period as "proudly individualistic towers of the nineteen-twenties and thirties, those 'cathedrals of commerce' and castles in the sky". This particular building was the headquarters of 'RCA' until that company moved to Rockefeller Center. The terracotta crown of the brick-tower was meant to symbolize "the radio waves and electric power of RCA".

L'ECHO DE PARIS

LEFT

Evening frocks from 'McCall's', April and July 1928. This American magazine featured the latest dress designs from Paris every month. A fashion editor's note tells you that smartly gowned young women filled the bustles on their evening gowns with tissue paper the colour of the fabric. "You know the trick by the crackle of the paper as they sit down." Paper patterns for all dresses illustrated in 'McCall's' were available at an average price of 45 cents. These patterns came in during the early 'twenties and were dictated by the rapidly diminishing clientele able to afford couturier's prices, and the ever-growing demand for fashionable but inexpensive clothes.

RIGHT

A standing cabinet inlaid with veneers in at least ten different kinds of wood, perhaps Portuguese. The stars are mother of pearl and the decoration round the coach lamp is inlaid brass. The scene depicts a lady in fancy dress standing in front of her carriage and obviously on the way to or from a 'bal masqué'. Fancy dress became very popular just after World War I; the Paris fashion designer Paul Poiret threw extravagant fancy-dress parties that were ruinously expensive. At least they helped to make his salon the most exclusive in Paris and set society on its path through the "roaring twenties".

RIGHT

Silver-plated modernist cocktail set with six cocktail goblets and a shaker; from the Paris workshop of Donald Desny. Classical Deco shapes are used here in designing containers for that classical Deco addiction, the cocktail. Here the novelty lies not in a joke idea but in streamlined modernism. The French designers produced some of the most elegant sets; for instance those that came from the Baccarat workshops with severe geometric patterns in black and white glass. Desny worked mostly in metal. There is a pure silver version of this set which sometimes comes with a matching glass and metal tray.

ABOVE
Cocktail cabinet by Maples of London dating from the 'thirties, with original decanters, glasses, cocktail shaker and lemon squeezer. This beautifully designed piece of furniture is in veneered maple wood with chrome fittings and blue mirror glass. The cocktail cabinet was a comparitively new piece of furniture, the mark of a changing society. Servants were no longer available to prepare elaborate dinner parties and the easiest way of entertaining was to invite people to cocktails. Most cocktail cabinets were designed to fit in with modernist interiors, but if a cabinet was required to fit into a room with antique furniture something suitable like an antique sideboard might be discreetly converted to conceal cocktail gear.

TOP RIGHT
A page from the 'Savoy Cocktail Book' complied by Harry Craddock, the barman at the Savoy Hotel, London. The book was published in 1930 with charming colour illustrations and decorations by Gilbert Rumbold. It contains everything the cocktail addict might need to know like the information that cocktails were named after "Coctel", the beautiful daughter of King Axolotl VIII of Mexico. It has recipes for

anything from a 'Bosom Caresser' to an 'Alabama Fizz' and it has a section entitled "a few hints for young mixers" – hint no. 4 is "shake the shaker as hard as you can: don't just rock it; you are trying to wake it up, not send it to sleep." The cocktail glasses and sticks date from the same period.

FAR RIGHT
Yellow glass cocktail shaker with hand-painted sunburst and cockerel decorations, and silver stopper and strainer combined with 1936 hallmark. The sunburst was perhaps the favourite English decorative device of the 'thirties; one associates it particularly with the glass in front doors of suburban homes or with enamelled compacts and cigarette cases, but it was very common in furniture and interior design of all sorts. There is a charming book called 'The English Sunrise' by Brian Rice and Tony Evans with a series of seventy-six photographs showing the sunrise as a decorative symbol. Most of the illustrations show designs dating from the 'twenties and 'thirties.

TOP FAR RIGHT
"The navy-blue ghost of Mr Blaker, the allegro negro cocktail-shaker": a quotation from 'Façade' by Edith Sitwell. The Negro cocktail shaker is used here as the design

for a combined table-lighter and cigarette dispenser by Ronson. The barman shakes away at a 'Fizz' behind his up-to-the-minute bar with its chrome streamlining and cocktail paraphernalia. The central section of the bar conceals a Ronson touch-tip lighter, and on each side the bar tops flip up to reveal a spring-loaded cigarette container. There was a whole series of these joke lighters. Another was designed so that, after pressing a lever, a slightly cubist monkey bent over to pick up a cigarette which had rolled out of a chrome and enamel dispenser.

RIGHT
English silver and enamel ladies' cigarette case (hallmarked 1931), with two dancing figures in brightly coloured costumes against a black background. On the back of the case there is a cherub in pink enamel on a blue background. The costumes are undoubtedly inspired by the work of Léon Bakst whose designs for ballets like 'Scheherezade' brought a middle Eastern look to Paris fashion for a while. Paul Poiret, whilst freeing women from their corsets, imprisoned them in hobble skirts. Although the baggy pantaloons on the cigarette case are reminiscent of the Kazbah, the zig-zags, cubes and geometric flowers, are pure European Art Deco.

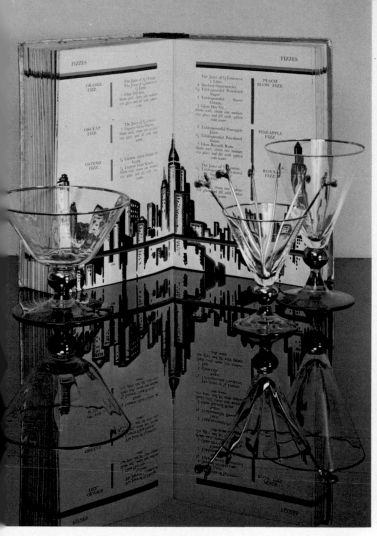

Decorative lamp by René Lalique (1860-1945). It has a moulded opaline glass body and elaborate stopper with acid-etched decoration of peacocks on a plastic base. Lalique was one of the most famous jewellery designers of the art noveau period, but with the growing pressures of commercialism gave this up and became a glass-designer. Although mass-produced, the glass is of an extremely high quality and beautifully designed. 'The Studio' of August 15th 1924 in appraising his work says "Lalique is raising moulded glass to a level which it has never before attained. By employing his moulds after the same fashion as a modeller in bronze employs those of a piece of sculpture Lalique secures effects similarly sculpturesque and opens up possibilities hitherto unexplored in this connection".

ACKNOWLEDGEMENTS

The publishers would like to thank the following for their kind permission to photograph the objects in this book:

Mr and Mrs Peter Alexander	14 right	Nigel Quiney	37 bottom, 53
Richard Rodney Bennett	13, 21	Michael Raeburn	19 top, 50 bottom
Brighton Museum	27, 28 top left & bottom right, 32 bottom, 37 top, 54 bottom	Sybarites Gallery, N.Y.	28 top right, 30 left, 38 top, 69 top
Butler & Wilson	17, 19 bottom, 25 bottom	Victoria and Albert Museum	endpapers, 23 bottom, 46 top right, 69, 72
Barrie Chilton	51 bottom		
Editions Graphiques	5, 22, 25 top	Peter Wentworth Shields	52 top, 59 bottom, 63 top
Martins Forrest, London	18 top, 26, 29, 30 right, 31, 44 top, 55, 71 bottom right		
Goldsmiths & Silversmiths Co Ltd	46 top left, 47		
Averil Hart	46 bottom right		
High Camp, London	6, 60 bottom		
Bevis Hillier	70		
Georg Jensen, London	45 top		
John Jesse	15, 45, 48, 58, 60 top		
Dan Klein	14 bottom, 16, 20, 23 top, 42, 43, 46 bottom left, 49, 52 bottom, 54 top, 58 inset, 59 top, 71		
John Lyons	56 left		
Diana & Simon Nicholson	12, 50 top		
L'Odeon, London	24, 51 top		

First Published 1974 by
Octopus Books Limited
59 Grosvenor Street, London W1
ISBN 0 7064 0323 1
© 1974 Octopus Books Limited
Produced by Mandarin Publishers Limited
14 Westlands Road, Quarry Bay, Hong Kong
Printed in Hong Kong